The Musical Collectibles of Raggedy Ann and Andy

by
Karen Kemp Shuttlesworth

AuthorHouse™
1663 Liberty Drive
Bloomington, IN 47403
www.authorhouse.com
Phone: 833-262-8899

Because of the dynamic nature of the Internet, any web addresses or links contained in this book may have changed since publication and may no longer be valid. The views expressed in this work are solely those of the author and do not necessarily reflect the views of the publisher, and the publisher hereby disclaims any responsibility for them.

Any people depicted in stock imagery provided by Getty Images are models, and such images are being used for illustrative purposes only. Certain stock imagery © Getty Images.

This book is printed on acid-free paper.

Photography: Karen Kemp Shuttlesworth
Artistic consultation: Lisa Coopersmith
Original art (back cover): Jim Kemp
Original poem: Amber Shuttlesworth

ORDERING INFO- www.authorhouse.com
Contact the author: RaggedyGG@hotmail.com

ISBN: 978-1-4259-6036-0 (sc)
ISBN: 978-1-4685-8986-3 (e)

Library of Congress Control Number: 2007903340

Print information available on the last page.

Published by AuthorHouse 11/15/2024

authorHOUSE®

Dedication

This work is lovingly dedicated to my mother, Dorothy Dean Dismukes Kemp (7 April 1926 - 7 September 2004). Her enduring love and support encouraged me to fulfill my dreams and career ambitions.

Special Thanks

I wish to thank my husband Kelley for providing me with the inspiration for the musical theme, supporting my collection obsession, and encouraging me by always being on the lookout for anything Raggedy!

A special thanks to Lisa Coopersmith, for her artistic contributions, support and friendship.

Important Message From The Author

Raggedy Ann is a fictional character created by Johnny Gruelle (1880-1938) in a series of books he wrote and illustrated for children. Originally hand crafted in 1915, the rag doll was introduced to the public in the 1918 book titled *Raggedy Ann Stories.* In 1920, the *Raggedy Andy Stories* were introduced, featuring Ann's brother. This book makes reference to the copyrighted characters and registered trademarks of Simon & Schuster, Inc. All rights reserved. All references are made solely for editorial purposes and neither the author nor the publisher makes any commercial claim to their use. Every effort has been made to ensure accuracy in the information provided at the time of publication.

TABLE OF CONTENTS

INTRODUCTION

Timeless. Classic. American icon. These are words commonly used to describe the irresistible rag doll created in the early 1900s by Johnny Gruelle. Raggedy Ann has been crowned one of the most popular dolls of the past century, reaching universality status among multiple generations. Fans of all ages love Raggedy Ann and Andy and the values that they represent. A number of guidebooks, magazines, newsletters, and Web sites are dedicated to this subject, offering collectors valuable product information and reference materials. Refer to the Internet Resources and Collector Guides sections for additional information and "must haves" for the Raggedy Fan!

What makes this book special? This illustrated treasury offers the reader a unique perspective — *The Music Collectibles of Raggedy Ann and Andy*. Music has the power to convey emotional meaning and connect people to one another. Music makes us better by stimulating our minds, touching our hearts, and helping us feel good about ourselves and the world. Raggedy Ann symbolizes love, kindness, generosity, and goodness, touching our hearts in so many ways. Raggedy Ann also has the power to provoke emotions and connect people to one another. Raggedy Ann and music—what a magical union! Johnny Gruelle recognized this connection as demonstrated in many of his literary works. Charming tales of fairies singing in the deep, deep woods, guests squeaking out sweet tunes at Hootie Owl's party, and Raggedy Ann playing the piano with her thumbs are just a few of the enchanting musical adventures we all love so much.

Inside, you'll find a cache of music collectibles, ranging from 1922 sheet music to a 2006 rocking chair musical doll. The wide array of toys, advertisements, music boxes, dolls, music mediums, sheet music, songbooks, and music works titled "Raggedy Ann" are sure to delight. I have used a very conservative approach in determining the Estimated Value (EV) for the collectibles featured in this publication. The acronyms used in the descriptions are:

- ♫ **EV:** Estimated Value
- ♫ **GC:** Good Condition
- ♫ **EC:** Excellent Condition
- ♫ **MIB:** Mint in Box (never opened)
- ♫ **NIB:** New in Box (opened but in excellent condition)
- ♫ **RV:** Retail Value (currently available on retail market)
- ♫ **HTF:** Hard to Find
- ♫ **DYK:** Did You Know? (interesting factoids)

May this illustrated treasury bring you reading pleasure and a new appreciation of how absolutely delightful it is to hear music from the heart of Raggedy Ann and Andy! Have yourself a magical musical raggedy day!

Karen (a.k.a. Raggedy*GG*)

ADVERTISEMENTS

Cover of 1973 Knickerbocker Toy Company catalog

M101a Ice Capades promotional booklet of the 1951 *Greatest Show on Ice* 11th Edition. (25 cents) Copyright 1930 (M101b) Back cover. (M101c) Raggedy Rhythm page. EV: $5

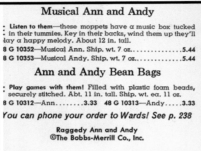

M166a The Montgomery Wards 1974 catalog page 302 features Musical Ann & Andy. "Listen to them—these moppets have a music box tucked to their tummies. Key in their backs, wind them up they'll play a happy melody." 12". The original price was $5.44. M166b Close up of dolls. M166c Page 302 features the 2-speed Portable Phonograph. Note the original price of $15.66.

M164a The Knickerbocker Toy Company 1973 retail catalog. (M164b) Page 22 features #3705 Raggedy Ann & Andy Musical Mobile.

2

M183a Advertisement from the JC Penney Christmas 1975 catalog featuring the Raggedy Ann and Andy Clock. M183b Close up. Note the original price of $14.66.

M167a The Montgomery Wards 1974 Catalog page 303 features Raggedy Ann portable radio. M167b Close up. Note the original price of $7.99.

M182a Advertisement from the JC Penney Christmas 1975 catalog page 345 featuring the Portable Radio Pal. Note the original cost of $6.97. M182b Close up of Portable Radio Pal ad.

M165 Knickerbocker Toy Company, Inc. 1968 retail catalog. Page 13 features Raggedy Ann and Andy Musical 15.5" dolls.

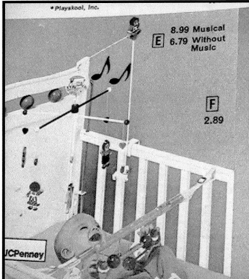

M15 Advertisement for Raggedy Ann and Andy Musical Mobile from the JC Penney Christmas catalog 1975. Hand painted wood base with figures. The mobile was available with or without a wind-up music box. Note the original price was $8.99. Mobile EV: $18-20 MIB $20-25

M104a Advertisement featuring 16" Knickerbocker Toy Company Raggedy Ann and Andy musical dolls from the 1970 Montgomery Ward's catalog. (M104b) Close up of Raggedy Ann and Andy. Note the 1970 price of $4.94 each for the musical doll and $5.88 for both of the non-musical dolls.

TOYS THAT TALK

☐ 8⁸⁸
ROW, ROW ROW YOUR BOAT

I'M YOUR POSTMAN
② 8⁴⁷

WHAT IS YOUR NAME? HOW OLD ARE YOU?
③ 3⁹⁹

HELLO. HOW ARE YOU?
④ 5⁹⁹

⑤ 6⁹⁷ each

See 'N Say® For Learning Fun

⑤ to ⑧ **Point the Dial to a Picture—Pull the Cord!** Talking pals tell kids all about their special worlds—from alphabet to nursery rhymes! Plastic stand-up base with carry handle. 10⅛ in. high. Ages 2 to 5.

[5] The Farmer Says. 12 animal names and sounds.
X 924-2892 A—Mail. wt. 2 lbs. 6.97
[6] The Bee Says. 26 alphabet letters and words.
X 924-2900 A—Mail. wt. 2 lbs. 6.97
[7] Raggedy Ann and Andy© Says. 12 household sayings.
See Raggedy Ann and Andy index, page 325.
X 923-8924 A—Mail. wt. 2 lbs. 6.97
[8] Mother Goose Says. 12 nursery rhyme phrases.
X 923-9047 A—Mail. wt. 2 lbs. 6.97
© Bobbs-Merrill Co., Inc.

M148 Advertisement for Raggedy Ann and Andy Says. The See N Say for Learning Fun Toys that talk from the JC Penney Christmas 1975 catalog. Note the original price was $6.97. See N Say EV: $75-100 HTF

① 19⁵⁰ 3-speed
② 14⁹⁹ 2-speed
③ 13⁹⁹ 2-speed

A GREAT GIFT VALUE
1-speed
Battery Operated!
Child never touches needle
④ 7⁹⁹

JCPenney 375

M184 Advertisement from the JC Penney Christmas 1975 catalog featuring the Raggedy Ann Portable 3- Speed Record Player. Note the original price of $19.50.

knickerbocker 1971
Toys for every age, for loving, for learning, for fun, forever!

1971 KNICKERBOCKER TOY CO. INC., N.Y. N.Y 10010

M60a Knickerbocker Toy Company 1971 catalog. The back cover (M60b) displays eight sizes of Raggedy Ann and Andy dolls, including the 15 ½ ' musical Ann and Andy. (M60c) Jump-N-Squeak Raggedy Ann (M60d) Jump-N-Squeak Raggedy Andy. EV: Priceless

RAGGEDY ANDY©
0003 — 15½"
0007 — 20"
0010 — 25½"
0012 — 31½"
0030 — 38½"
0014 — 45"

RAGGEDY ANN©
0001 — 15½"
0005 — 20"
0008 — 25½"
0011 — 31½"
0029 — 38½"
0013 — 45"

0303 — MUSICAL©
15½"

0301 — MUSICAL©
15½"

knickerbocker Toy co, inc

9260 — JUMP-N-SQUEAK ASST.® —
5 each 1001, 4 each 1003, 3 each 1080; 9".

JUMP-N-squeak
RAGGEDY ANN
PULL HERE

1001 — JUMP-N-SQUEAK RAGGEDY ANN®

1003 — JUMP-N-SQUEAK RAGGEDY ANDY®

Talking Gift Pak III
Enchanting 3-D color stories of Charlie Brown, Star Trek, Bazooka Joe, Scoobie Doo, Tom Sawyer, and Casper the Ghost with SOUND NARRATIONS

13⁹⁹
6 reels included

GAF TALKING VIEW-MASTER® GIFT PAK. Great fun! Hold up to light and press sound bar to hear narrated 3-D scenes. You get talking viewer, 6 talking reels (42 scenes), and canister. Uses 2 "C" batteries (not incl.).
X 918-8236 A—Mailing weight 2.75 lbs. 13.99

M95 Advertisement for GAF Talking View Master-The Gift Pak. Hold up to the light and press the sound bar to hear narrated 3-D scenes. From the JC Penney 1975 Christmas Catalog. Note the original price was $13.99. Raggedy Ann View Master packets were sold separately, along with Cinderella, Charlie Brown and Winnie the Pooh. View Master EV: $10-15

M110 Playbill featuring "Raggedy Ann The Musical Adventure" performed at the Nederlander Theatre in New York City on October 6, 1986. Music and lyrics by Joe Raposo.

♫ **DYK:** In Jan 2006 a See N Say with crayon marks in non working condition sold on Ebay for $152.

MUSIC BOXES

Raggedy Ann says, "Play It Again, Andy"

♫ **DYK:** The origin of music boxes dates back to the 14th century when a bell ringer invented a cylinder with pins which operated cams, which then hit the bells.

 M8 Raggedy Ann and Andy ceramic music box. Made by Sankyo, Price Imports, Japan. 1968-1972. Plays *"Raindrops Keep Falling On My Head"* or *"This Old Man"*. EV: $12-15 *Raindrops Keep Falling On My Head* lyrics can be found @ http://www.searchlyrics.org *This Old Man* lyrics can be found @ www.niehs.nih.gov/kids/lyrics/oldman.htm

 M136 Ann and Andy music box spins around as it plays tune # 263 *"The Candy Man"*. Schimd Bros, Inc. Made in Japan 1973 by The Bobbs-Merrill Company, Inc. EV: $12-15

♫ **DYK:** *The Candyman* song was used in the original "Willy Wonka and the Chocolate Factory" and was also performed by Sammy Davis Jr.

♫ **DYK:** The first musical box (or music box) was produced in 1811 in Sainte-Croix.

  M11a Raggedy Andy musical mug. The 4" ceramic mug plays *"Chim Chiminey"* tune when the mug is lifted. M11b Bottom of mug with musical turn key. Made by Schimd in Japan 1971 for The Bobbs-Merrill Company, Inc. EV: $8-10

♫ **DYK:** *Chim Chiminey* lyrics were written by Richard M. Sherman and Robert B. Sherman (a popular tune from the movie *Mary Poppins*). Lyrics can be found at www.niehs.nih.gov/kids/lyrics/chim.htm

 M32 Raggedy Ann Musical Mug. The 4" ceramic mug plays *"A Spoonful of Sugar"* tune # 143 when lifted. Also available with Ann & Andy. Plays tune *"Hi Lily Hi Lily Hi Lo"* Made 1971 in Japan by Schimd Bros. for The Bobbs-Merrill Company, Inc. EV: $10-12

 M12 Raggedy Ann and Andy music box. Ann and Andy playing with toys, wood base is 6" with cloth clothing. Swiss movement. Arms and heads move with tune. Made 1971 in Italy by ANRI for Bobbs-Merrill, Co. Inc. Tune: Toy Land. EV: $35-40

 M13 Raggedy Ann and Andy ceramic music box. Made in Japan 1971 by Schimd for The Bobbs-Merrill Company, Inc. Plays the *"Do-Re-Mi"* tune. EV: $20-25

 M35 Raggedy Andy figurine by Bobbs-Merrill, Co. Inc for Schmid # 1071. Measures 8". A sticker on the underside reads *"Do Re Mi"* tune. EV: $12-15

♫ **DYK:** The term "music box" actually refers to the mechanical elements which produce the movement & music. Today music boxes can be found in watches, books, greeting cards, dolls, toys, key chains, jewelry boxes and many other novelty items.

♫ **DYK:** Schmid closed in 1995 increasing the interest in the company's collectibles. The values of certain items especially the musical pieces continue to rise.

M19 Raggedy Ann and Andy musical bank. Ceramic 4 ½" No markings. Music plays when coin in inserted. The back has wooden panel and winder. Key winder reads "ToYo". Tune: *"Somewhere My Love".* EV: $12-15

♫ **DYK:** *"Somewhere My Love"* is also known as *"Lara's Theme"* or *"Love Theme"* from the movie Dr. Zhivago. Lyrics by Francis Paul Webster

M21 Raggedy Ann and Andy music box. Ceramic on plastic base. Sticker- Made in Japan. Manufacturer Pat P. Two sizes, on left: 7 ½", on right 6". Some play the theme from *"Love Story"*, others play *"School Days"* or *"Lara's Theme".* EV: GC $15-20

M23 Raggedy Ann Santa Music Box. 8" plastic turns as the music plays *"Twelve Days of Christmas"*. Made 1972-1973 in Japan by Berman and Anderson, Inc. EV: $12-15

♫ **DYK:** The Love Story lyrics were written by Carl Sigman and music by France Lai and best known from the movie, Love Story released in 1970. The movie received seven Academy Award nominations and won an Oscar for Francis Lai's original music score.

♫ **DYK:** Twelve Days of Christmas has a French origin from the 1770's. The twelve days refer to the days between the birth of Christ (25 December) and the coming of Magi (Epiphany 6 January).

M33 Raggedy Ann and Andy Music Box. Action Lobeco ceramic box rotates and the see-saw moves up and down while the music plays *"Rockabye Baby"* or *"Raindrops Keep Falling on my Head"*. Made in Japan 1960's. EV: $15-20

M34 Raggedy Ann and Andy "School Days, School Days, Dear Old Golden Rule Days" music box. Plays *"School Days"* tune. 6.5" tall. Made in Japan 1972 by Chadwick-Miller. EV: $15-18

♫ **DYK:** *"School Days"* was a 1957 hit record by singer/songwriter Chuck Berry epitomizing the attitudes of high school students of that time. www.school-for-champions.com

♫ **DYK:** Music boxes were the precursor to jukeboxes!

M69a Raggedy Ann Jewelry Music Box. # 1665. Plays *"Raindrops Keep Falling On My Head"*. Made 1972 by Durham Industries, Inc NY, NY for Bobbs-Merrill Co., Inc. Made in Japan #1665. M69b Inside: the plastic flower spins as music plays. EV: $18-20

M70a Raggedy Ann and Andy Jewelry Music Box. "A place to keep your treasures". M70b Ann spins around as tune plays *"Dance Ballerina Dance"*. 2003 Made in China by Schylling for Simon Schuster Inc. The music box is decorated with Volland looking dolls and inspirational phrases like, "Happiness is very easy to catch." RV: $18

M77 Raggedy Ann and Andy Flying High music box. 6" Ceramic with metal on and off lever on the rear. Ann and Andy sit in a plane atop a white cloud decorated with yellow stars. Limited Edition of 10,000 by Schimd 1982 Plays *"Love Will Keep Us Together"* EV: $50-60 HTF

M78 Pair of Raggedy Ann and Andy musical figurines. Plays *"My Favorite Things"* from *"The Sound of Music"*. 4" tall. 1999 San Francisco Music Box & Gift Co. Simon & Schuster. RV: $12 each.

♫ **DYK:** Toni Tennille and Daryl Dragon "The CAPTAIN and TENILLE" released their first album in 1974 and it rocketed to stardom shortly thereafter, taking top honors at the 1975 Grammy Awards winning Record of the Year for "Love Will Keep Us Together." Toni and Daryl first heard this song when Kip Cohen, vice president of A&M, called them into his office and played the song from a Neil Sedaka album recorded a year earlier! http://www.superseventies.com/1975_1singles.html

M81a Raggedy Ann musical Skating Pond. Snowden swirls and twirls around the pond to *"We Wish You A Merry Christmas"* M81b Pond close up. 1998 Snowden Collection sold exclusively at Target. Original price: $19.99. EV: $20-25 NIB $30

M82 Raggedy Ann musical ceramic bank measures 6 ¼" tall and plays *"High Lily High Low"*. Music plays tune when coin is inserted. 1976. M.I.M. Lador, Inc. New York. EV: $15-18

M83 Raggedy Ann and Andy musical pair. Measure 3 ½" wide x 6 ¼" tall. Raggedy Ann plays *"This Old Man"*. Andy plays *"The Love Story"*. Made in Japan. Original Artmart. 1970's. EV: $20-25 for the pair.

M84 Raggedy Ann and Andy Sharing a Hug porcelain bell. Made by The Bobbs-Merrill Company, Inc. for Schmid Bros 1971. The Schmid paper label is attached on the inside of the bell cavity. EV: $10-12

M85 Raggedy Ann Music Box. Porcelain plays *"Toy Land"* while Ann and Teddy slowly turn. 1980-1982 by Schimd in Taiwan, Musical Collectibles Taiwan for The Bobbs-Merrill Company, Inc. EV: $12-15

♪ **DYK:** *"Toy Land"* is an adaptation from Babes in Toyland, one of the most beloved operettas of all time. Music was written by Victor Herbert Libretto. Lyrics written by Glenn MacDonough in the early 1900s. Lyrics can be found at www.kididdles.com

M89 Raggedy Ann and Andy musical house. Plays *"Oh What a Beautiful Morning"* as the pathway revolves clockwise. Made by Enesco. Measures 11" tall by 10" wide. Ann and Andy wave from the window. Turn pathway to wind up. A switch turns the music on and off. Made of wood. EV: $30-35

M96 Raggedy Ann and Andy music box # 225991. Plays *"Let Me Call You Sweetheart"* San Francisco Gift Co. Simon & Schuster 2004. Made in China. EV: $20-25

♪ **DYK:** Rueben also made a Ferris wheel music box planter # 3235

M98 Raggedy Andy playing upright piano ceramic planter. 1976 The Bobbs-Merrill Company, Inc. With the turn of a side knob plays the theme song *"Raggedy Ann & Andy"* EV: $8-10

M120 Raggedy Ann ceramic music box piano planter #4187M by The Bobbs-Merrill Company, Inc. 5"x5" 1/8" x 4 ¾" With the turn of a side knob plays the theme song *"Raggedy Ann & Andy"* 1976-1978 Made in Japan for Ruben Collectibles Los Angeles, CA. EV: $10-12

M100a Raggedy Ann musical jewelry box by Durham Industries for Bobbs-Merrill, Co. Inc., 1972. Made in Japan. (b) Inside view. Plays *"Raindrops Keep Falling On My Head"*. Measures 9" by 3.5 ". EV: $12-15

M121a Porcelain music box by Flambro with paper tags and original box. Plays *"It's a Small World"* TM Macmillan. Made in Malaysia 1980's. M121b close up. Some models play *"You've Got a Friend"*. EV: EC $18 MIB $25

M122a Revolving Musical Raggedy Kid Decoration with the original box. Handcrafted in Hong Kong. The original retail price was $7.99. M122b Close up of box. Made by Commodore Manufacturing Corp. Brooklyn NY. 1960-70's Music mechanism made by Sankyo, Japan. 7 ½ inches tall. Plays *"Jingle Bells"* written by James Pierpont. EV: $15-18 MIB $20-25

M124 Holiday Jamboree Snowden & Friends Christmas animated music box with the original box. Target exclusive 1998. Distributed by Dayton Hudson Corporation Minneapolis, MN. Made in China. The original retail price was $49.99. Snowden leads the music with Raggedy Ann & Andy joining in the duet. Their forest friends sing along to create a charming scene. Plays 20 Christmas carols. EV: $25-30 MIB $45

M125　Raggedy Ann and Andy Musical Figurine. They go up and down on the teeter totter when the music plays. The tune is *"Have Yourself a Merry Little Christmas"* Measures 6". Kurt S. Adler Simon & Schuster, Inc. EV: $25-30

M127 Raggedy Andy on Red Bicycle Christmas theme music box. 1980's Schmid EV: $15-20

♫ **DYK:** The tune *"Have Yourself a Merry Little Christmas"* has been recorded by Christina Aguilera, Amy Grant, Garth Brooks, Lone Star and Whitney Houstan.

M138a Complete Raggedy Ann Orchestra 8 piece collection. "Music Makes Our Hearts Sing". Inspired by the original Raggedy Ann Stories. Limited Edition by Simon & Schuster, Inc. Made in China by Enesco 2001 RV: $10-15 each. Upper left: #864927 "Our Friendship Has A Special Beat" Raggedy Ann With Symbols Figurine and #864919 "Music Is The Laughter In Our Hearts" Raggedy Andy With Accordion Figurine.

M138c #864943 "Friendship Is The Rhythm Of Life" Marcella The Conductor Figurine.

M138d #864935 "A Melody is A Memory In Our Hearts" Raggedy Ann With Flute Figurine.

M138e #864978 "Whenever You're Near, Sweet Music I Hear" Raggedy Ann & Andy With Cello Figurine.

M138g #868744 "Music Brings Friends Together" Raggedy Andy Playing Saxophone With Wrinkled Knee Camel

M138h #864951 "Everything Sounds Better, When We Play Together" Raggedy Ann & Andy With Piano Figurine.

M138f #864986 "Together We Make A Beat That Makes You Tap Your Feet" Raggedy Ann With Trumpet & Andy With Drum Figurine.

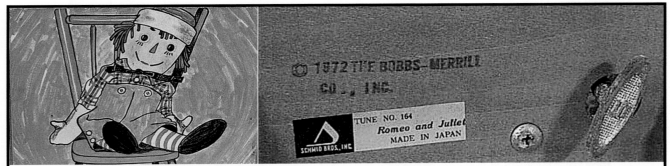

M133a Raggedy Andy music box by Schimd 1972. Plays tune: *"Romeo and Juliet"* M133b Bottom of box showing paper label and turn key. EV: $15-18

M142 Raggedy Ann and Andy Lucky Pennies music box. Made by the San Francisco Music Box Company. 2004-2005 Ann standing and Andy sitting on a grassy knoll of flowers. Measures 5" tall x 5 ½ " wide. The back of book reads Raggedy Ann's Lucky Pennies. Written and illustrated by Johnny Gruelle. The poem on the book reads: *May Your Pathway through the Deep, Deep Woods of Life be filled with the Sunshine of happiness and bordered with the Flowers of Love and with Lucky Penny Trees.* Plays the tune *"That's What Friends Are For".* EV: $20-22

♫ **DYK:** The tune, *"That's What Friends Are For"* was written by Burt Bacharach and Carole Bayer Sager.

M143 Raggedy Ann and Andy Music Box. Patchwork Horse. Made by the San Francisco Music Box Co. 2004-2005 Raggedy Ann and Andy are riding a little patch work horse on a green knoll with flowers. Plays tune: *"Playmate".* Words and music written by Saxie Dowell. Copyright 1940 by Santly-Joy-Select, Inc. Measures 6 ¼" tall x 4" wide. EV: $15-18

M144 Raggedy Ann and Andy Musical Snow Globe. Made by San Francisco Music Box Company 2004-2005. Ann and Andy are in a row boat on the water inside the globe. The globe is sitting on a hill surrounded by flowers and lucky pennies. Plays tune *"Let Me Call You Sweetheart".* Measures 7" tall x 6 ½" wide. EV: $12-15

M160a Raggedy Ann music box by Russ Berrie, Inc. Memories Are For Sharing, Celebrating 90 years. Plays an instrumental virtuoso piano music by Beethoven, *"Fur Elise".* Simon and Schuster, Inc. 2005. Made of resin, item No. 38079. M160b Removable top reveals a small compartment for storage of tiny treasures and trinkets! RV: $15

DOLLS

My favorite doll, a Joy of a Toy Knickerbocker,
pictured in the 1968 KTC catalog and autographed by Ruth Gruelle.

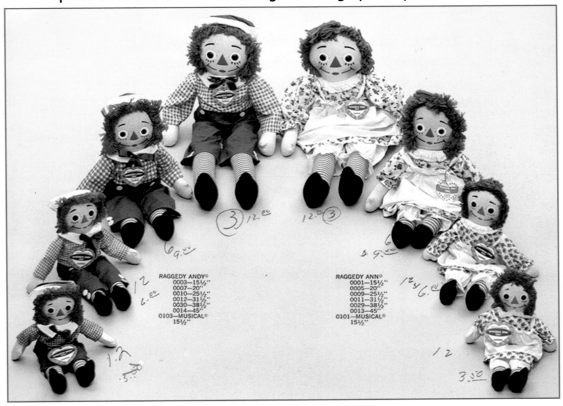

Raggedy Ann and Andy

I have a lot of rag dolls all through out my home,
Each a different shape and size, with a personality of its own.
Some are more recent, while others are very old,
I have quite a collection, or so I have been told.

They start out in my kitchen, and fill the foyer and the halls,
Some are scattered around the table
And others hang on the walls.
I have everything there is from dolls, toys, and books.
Raggedy Ann and Andy fill the corners, crannies and nooks.

With all these Anns and Andys, what's a girl to do?
Go looking for more of course to add something new.
Raggedy Ann and Andy little faces that shine so bright,
Waiting for me to come and adopt them, and you know....
I just might!

Written by Amber Shuttlesworth
22 March 2000

M18 Raggedy Ann musical (red poppy flowered dress) doll. Plays *"Rock-a Bye Baby"* 15". Made in Hong Kong by the Knickerbocker Toy Company (KTC) 1964 Myrtle Gruelle. EV: GC $35-45 EC with apron/tag $75 MIB $100 or more.

♫ **DYK:** KTC was the first manufacturer of musical dolls 1963-1982. During this period dolls were made with five different mouth variations, five eye variations, and three different "I Love You" variations on the chest. There were ten different tags all attached to the clothing (usually the apron) not the doll itself. Unfortunately the apron is often missing. MacMillan Co. made a 25" musical pair in 1986. Applause made a 15" musical pair.

♫ **DYK:** *"Rock a Bye Baby"* is also known as *"Hush a Bye Baby"*. Lyrics can be found @ www. niehs.nih.gov/kids/lyrics/rockaby.htm

♫ **DYK:** The origin of the words to *"Rock a Bye Baby"* lie deep in American history dating back to the 1700's. Native Indian mothers would suspend a birch bark cradle from the branches of a tree, enabling the wind to rock the cradle and the child to sleep. www.rhymes.org.uk/ rock_a_a_bye_baby.htm

M67a Raggedy Andy Get Well doll. Doll is 8" inside a gift box. Press his belly and hear the music *"You Are My Sunshine"*. Applause/Hasbro 2003. Made in China. M67b Doll close up. RV: $16

♫ **DYK:** *"You Are My Sunshine"* was written by former Louisiana State Governor Jimmie Davis and Charles Mitchell; copyright 1940 and 1977 by Peer International Corporation. This song with ten verses is one of two official songs for the State of Louisiana.

M68a Raggedy Ann Get Well doll. Doll is 8" inside a gift box. Press her belly and hear the music *"You Are My Sunshine"* Applause/Hasbro 2003 Made in China. M68b Heart close up. RV: $16

M73a Raggedy Ann Birthday Wishes doll. Press her belly and hear "*The Happy Birthday*" song. Doll is 8" in a gift box that can be personalized with a handwritten message. 2003 Hasbro/Applause. Made in China. M73b Doll close up. M73c Box close up RV: $16

M74a Raggedy Andy Birthday Wishes doll. Press his belly and hear "*The Happy Birthday*" song. Doll is 8" in a gift box that can be personalized. 2003 Hasbro/Applause. Made in China. M74b Doll close up. RV: $16

♫ **DYK:** The National Toy Hall of Fame was established in 1998 by A, C. Dilbert's Discovery Village, a children's museum in Salem, Oregon to recognize toys that have achieved longevity and national significance in the world of play and imagination. The permanent home for the Hall of Fame is now in Rochester, NY. Raggedy Ann was voted into The National Toy Hall of Fame in March 2002.

M79a Raggedy Ann musical (blue and green poppy flowered dress) 15½" doll. Tag reads "Joy of a Toy" Made in Hong Kong. Plays "*Rock-a-Bye-Baby*". Knickerbocker Toy Co. 1967-1983. M79b Front of tag. M79c Back of tag. M79d Music turn key. EV: *GC* $25-30 EC $45-50 MIB $75.00+

18

M111a Raggedy Andy musical doll. 15 ½" Plays *"Frere Jacques"* Joy of a Toy Knickerbocker Toy Co. Middlesex, NJ. Made in Taiwan The Republic of China. Label on back of suit. 1967-1969. M111b Label front. M111c label back.

♫ **DYK:** Frere Jacques translated to English means "Are You Sleeping?"

M119 Raggedy Andy musical doll by Applause A Division of Wallace Berry Co. Inc. Woodhills, CA 1986 McMillan, Inc. Made in Taiwan Item # 847. The head rotates to the tune *"Raindrops Keep Falling On My Head"*. A Raggedy Ann version was also made. She has a blue dress with red polka dots and white apron! EV: GC $30-35 fully clothed. EC pair with original tags $75-80.

M151a Raggedy Andy musical doll. The Knickerbocker Toy Company 1976. Plays *"Mary Had A Little Lamb."* M151b Doll close up. EV: GC $12-15 EC $25-30

♫ **DYK:** *Mary Had Little Lamb* was written by Sarah Josepha Hale, editor of Godey's Lady's Book, 1830's.

M152a Raggedy Andy- no tie. Plays *"Rock a Bye Baby"*. Same variation of eyes, eye lashes, mouth and "I Love You" heart as M111 only a little more loved! Missing pant buttons and ribbon bow tie. M152b Label front. M152c Label back. EV: *GC $20 EC $35 MIB $75+*

♫ **DYK:** Raggedy Ann was ranked #12 of the favorite American toys and games of the 20th century. Over 13,000 votes cast....see website: http://biz.yahoo.com/prnews/991101/va_buck_1.html .

TOYS

"Beloved Belindy and the Camel with Wrinkled Knees ready to jam!"

♪ DYK: The concept of "Toys for Tots" began in 1947 with a handcrafted Raggedy Ann doll! Visit www.toysfortots.org for a complete history of this foundation that has touched the lives of more than 160 million children.

M1a Portable Radio Pal. AM radio with colorful plastic case and carrying strap. 2 ¼ inch dynamic speakers and earphones for private listening. Plastic radio size is 6" x 5" and requires a 9 -volt battery. Made in Hong Kong 1973 by Philgee International, LTD for The Bobbs-Merrill Company, Inc. M1b Radio close up. See M182a,b for advertisement. EV: GC $20-25 MIB $30- 40

M4 Play Along Xylophone. Play tunes with four colorful disks and follow along with songbook. Battery operated, metal and plastic, 9 ½"x6 ½"x6 ½". Made in 1978 by Azrak-Hamilton, Inc for Bobbs-Merrill. EV: GC $35-40 MIB $55-65 HTF

M9 Raggedy Ann Sing-A-Long Radio. It's an AM radio, sing-a-long and PA system. Flower shaped microphone. Plastic 7"x7", 1975 by Concept 2000 for Bobbs-Merrill, Co. Inc. EV: $30-40

M14a Ann on wind-up musical Rocking Horse. M14b Andy. Plays *"Oh Suzanna"*. An Illco Preschool 6 ½" toy made in Hong Kong for Ill Felder Toy Co. for Bobbs-Merrill, Co. Inc. 1975. EV: $20-25 each

M16 Raggedy Ann and Andy Clock. A 30-hour wind-up clock that requires one "C" battery. Made 1975 in Hong Kong. Instead of an alarm, the characters on face wake the kids up by talking to them. See M183a & b for advertisement. EV: $20-25 MIB $50-75

M20 Chime Ball. (Sometimes referred to as a rattle). 1974 Bobbs-Merrill Co., Inc. Available with red or blue bottom. Sold on eBay for $32 in April 2005. EV: GC $8-10

M17a Raggedy Ann and Andy Portable 3-Speed Record Player. The 7" turntable has 3 speeds and built in 45rpm adapter. Vinyl-clad hardboard cabinet with hinged cover and plastic handle. Made 1972-74 by Vanity Fair # 104 for Bobbs-Merrill Company, Inc. M17b Close up. See M184 for advertisement. EV: GC $40-45 MIB $50-60

M22a Big Sounder Solid State Phonograph. The plastic heart shaped player is battery operated and uses 33 1/3 and 45 rpm records. Made in Japan by Janex Corp in 1972-1975 for Bobbs-Merrill Co., Inc. Requires two "D" batteries to operate. M22b inside view. EV: GC $35-40 MIB $50-60

M26 Raggedy Ann and Andy Musical Lamp. Judy Originals. Wooden lamp base with wooden Ann and Andy playing ball. The red ball winds-up and plays *"Playmates"*. 1980. EV: $ 25-30 *"Playmates"* words and music written by Saxie Dowell. Copyright 1940 by Santley-Joy- Select Inc.

M30 Tambourine. 6" round no model #. Made in 1973 by Kingsway for Bobbs-Merrill Company, Inc. EV: GC $15 EC $20

M71a Raggedy Ann Piano Book. # J4335. Book has 15 numbered piano keys that allow the user to play the 10 song tunes. By JAYMAR for the Bobbs-Merrill Company, Inc. Made in Japan. MCMLXXII (1972) Ten song titles; M71b close up of *Three Blind Mice.* Also includes *Pop Goes the Weasel, Mary had a Little Lamb, Twinkle Twinkle Little Star, Jingle Bells, London Bridges, Sing a Song of Sixpence, Swanee River, Long, Long Ago* and *Home Sweet Home.* EV: $45 MIB $65-75

M72 Raggedy Ann and Andy Playtime Song Book. Just press the button on the keypad and sing along. Replaceable long-life batteries included. Retailed for $16.95 in 2002. Publications International, Ltd. Simon & Schuster. EV: $12-15.

Song Titles: A Bicycle Built for Two; Camptown Races; She'll Be Coming Around the Mountain; My Bonnie Lies Over the Ocean; One, Two Buckle My Shoe; Pop! Goes the Weasel; Skip to My Lou; Where Has My Little Dog Gone? What are Little Boys made Of? Twinkle, Twinkle Little Star

♪ **DYK:** Replacement batteries can be ordered from Publications International, LTD., Dept B24, P.O. Box 8093 Wisconsin Rapids, WI 54495-8093. Offer good only in US.

M75 Raggedy Ann and Andy Favorite Things lapel pins made of soft flexible PVC. (left) Raggedy Andy with Guitar item #80 RA011 measures $1\frac{1}{4}$" x $\frac{3}{4}$". (right) Raggedy Ann Singing item #80 RA006 measures $1\frac{1}{2}$" x $\frac{3}{4}$" Made in China 2006. Simon & Schuster, Inc. Licensed by United Media. RV: $4 each.

M76a Raggedy Ann and Andy Dancing music box. 4"x4" More fun from Schylling. Simon & Schuster. Made in China 2001. Licensed by United Media 2003. M76b Close up. Plays *"Twinkle Twinkle Little Star"*. Lyrics written by Jane Taylor in 1806. RV: $16.99. You can hear this song at www.niehs.nih.gov/kids/lyrics/twinkle.htm

M88 Raggedy Ann and Andy wooden music box. 1975 The Bobbs-Merrill, Company, Inc. Inside rotates with view through cut out window. Made in Japan. Plays Tune # 201 *"Theme From Love Story"* EV: $50-65

M90 Raggedy Ann Musical Rocker by Russ Berrie and Company, Inc. Made in China. 2006. Plays *"Rock-A-Bye Baby"* Ann is dressed in the traditional red, white and blue colors with apron riding a wooden horse. Squeeze her hand to activate. Doll measures 12" tall. RV: $10-12

M91 Raggedy Ann Lollipop Chime Doll. 2005 Simon & Schuster. Rocks from side to side with a chiming sound. Russian Folk crafted similar to the Nesting dolls. RV: $20

M97 Raggedy Ann and Andy (referred to as the See Saw or Teeter Totter) lamp. 1973 by The Bobbs-Merrill Company, Inc. Plays *"Playmate"* or *"Rock-a-Bye Baby"* as the see saw moves up and down. Turn the red ball to start the music. EV: $15-18

M108a Classic Tales Raggedy Ann and Raggedy Andy 1971 View Master (3 reel) 21 Stereo Pictures Packet # B 406 The Bobbs-Merrill Company, Inc. M108b GAF Corporation with 16 page color illustrated booklet. Each reel has 7 full color three dimension pictures. (1) Raggedy Ann Learns a Lesson (2) Raggedy Andy Arrives (3) Doctor Raggedy Andy. EV: $5-7

M113 Raggedy Ann musical doll face toy 1975 The Bobbs-Merrill Company, Inc. Pull string and plays *"Hello Dolly"* Has string for hanging. Music and lyrics were written by Jerry Herman. EV: $35-40 HTF

M115 The Original Adventures of Raggedy Ann & Andy jingle cloth block with original tag. 5" The Toy Works Middle Falls, NY 1991 Macmillan Co. Inc. Made in USA. The six sides feature pictures from the book of same name. EV: $35-45

♫ **DYK:** One of the most popular Broadway musicals ever written, *Hello Dolly* opened at the St. James Theater in New York City on January 16, 1964 and ran for 2,844 performances becoming the longest running musical for its time.

M116a Classic Raggedy Ann and Andy Musical Mobile. Mobile rotates as it plays *"Brahms Lullaby"*. Universal mount fits most cribs. Use only for babies 0-5 months. On/off switch on box. M116b soft lush characters Raggedy Ann, white Raggedy dog, and yellow duck with blue bonnet on! Made by Simon and Schuster 2003. EV: $10-12

M134a Ann and Andy yellow mirror baby toy is a delightful musical noise maker. 1976 Bobbs-Merrill, Co. Inc., Stahlwood Toy N.Y. 10019 EV: $4-6

M134b Ann baby rattle noise maker. 1974 The Bobbs-Merrill Company Inc. Made in Hong Kong. EV: $4-6

M118 Raggedy Ann "Jack in the Box" More Fun From Schylling. Simon and Schuster Inc., Licensed by United Media. 2003. Plays *"Pop Goes the Weasel"*. Lyrics can be found at www. niehs.nih.gov/kids/lyrics/weasle.htm RV: $25

M153 Raggedy Andy Rattle in original package. For ages up to 18 months. The Bobbs-Merrill Company, Inc. 1974 Made in Hong Kong. EV: $6-8

M145a Show 'N Tell Picturesound Program made by Child Guidance Playthings, Inc., a subsidiary of Gabriel Industries, Inc Bronx, NY in 1978 for The Bobbs-Merrill Company, Inc. M145b Raggedy Ann and Andy and the Singing Shell Record and Film Strip # 51474. Additional series available # 51475 Raggedy Ann and Andy and the Kite, #51476 Raggedy Ann and Andy and the Kittens. M145c Close up of record. EV: $12-15

M154a Raggedy Ann & Andy Musical Toothbrush in original package. 1975 The Bobbs-Merrill Company, Inc. Jingles as you brush your teeth! M154b Close up of back of package. M154c Close up of toothbrush. EV: GC in original package $12-15. Without package $8-10

MADE IN HONG KONG   NO.353K
© 1977 THE BOBBS-MERRILL COMPANY INC.
© STAHLWOOD TOY MFG. CO. INC., N.Y. 10019

M156a Trio of Raggedy Andy and Ann squeaky toys. 6 inches. M156 b & c (two on left) were made in Taiwan Stahlwood Toy New York. 1981 The Bobbs-Merrill Company Inc. M156d (far right) has slightly different eyes. Only marking is "Taiwan" but appears to be a Bobbs-Merrill, perhaps a different production year. EV: $5 each

M157 Ann holding guitar, hard rubber composite measuring 4.5 inches. No markings. On the bottom is a horizontal open slot as if it attached to something else. EV: $5-7

M158 Andy rattle 5 inches. 1974 The Bobbs-Merrill Company, Inc. Stahlwood Toy New York. Made in Hong Kong. Attached to a suction cup for play. EV: $5-7

M161 Raggedy Ann and Andy AM Radio with plastic hand strap. 1974 The Bobbs-Merrill Company, Inc. Requires 9 volt battery. Philgee International LTD. Made in Hong Kong. EV: $20-25.

M163 Raggedy Ann & Andy Shoe Ties. "Keeps Child's Laces Securely Tied" Know where your baby is at all times by listening to the jingling bells! 1978 The Bobbs-Merrill Company Inc. Stahlwood Toy Mfg Co. Inc. New York. Made in Hong Kong. Original package unopened. EV: $20-25 HTF

M126 Raggedy Ann and Andy A Musical Adventure. A Dell Yearling Special. An adaptation by Kathleen N. Daly of Patricia Thackray's and Max Wilk's screenplay for the animated film, "A Musical Adventure". 1977 The Bobbs-Merrill Company Inc. Original retail price $2.95.

M169a Raggedy Andy musical key chain. M169b Wind up key on back, with a "clover like" engraved symbol and sticker which reads Made in Japan. Appears to be from the 1970's perhaps Bobbs-Merrill. Tune unknown. EV: $10-12

M31a Raggedy Ann and Andy Musical Mobile. Made 1980 by Dolly Toy Co. for The Bobbs-Merrill Company, Inc. Plays *"Brahms' Lullaby"*. M31b, c features puffed fabric characters of Ann, Andy, elephant, dog and lion. EV: $20-25 MIB $30-35

♫ **DYK:** Brahms' Lullaby (also known as Lullaby and Goodnight) was written by Johannes Brahms. Lyrics can be found at http://kididdles.com

MUSIC MEDIUMS

"Ann relaxing in the music room listening to her favorite stories on CD."

M2a A Raggedy Ann Song Book (33rpm record). The tunes of "The Raggedy Ann's Sunny Songs". Performed by the Richard Wolfe Children's Chorus. Recorded in RCA's Studio C, New York City. 1971 RCA Records, NY, NY. Printed in U.S.A. Cover art by Ollie Alpert is an interpretation of the original drawings by Johnny Gruelle. M2b book back shows song titles: My Raggedy Ann, The Cheery Scarecrow, The Fairy Ring, The Worn Out Doll, The Cookie Bush, Mother Dear, Johnny Cricket, Fredericka, The Singing Brooklet, Little Wooden Willie, The Tired Old Horse, The Camel with the Wrinkled Knees, Magic Songs of Happiness, Coo Coo Clock, Snoopwiggy, Happy Bluebird, Raggedy Andy, Happy Toad, The Hootie Owls. EV: $10-12

M3 Raggedy Ann Sunny Songs. A three -78rpm record set. Music by Will Woodin (1868-1934). Lyrics by Johnny Gruelle. Sung by Frank Luther. 1946 Decca Records # A- 494. Album case contains a Union label stamp: International Brotherhood of Bookbinders. Made in U.S.A. EV: $15-18

♫ **DYK:** A soft cover "Raggedy Ann Song Book" was also published which contained the words to the above songs. Piano arrangements by John Lane.

♫ **DYK:** A Raggedy Ann Sunny Songs 12 page booklet was also published by Decca Records in 1946. The book cover is very similar to the record album cover. It provides information about Frank Luther, Johnny Gruelle and the lyrics to songs such as "The Cheery Scarecrow", "The Worn Out Doll", "The Cookie Bush", "Beloved Belindy", "Fredricka", and "The Tired Old Horse".

♫ **DYK:** In 1944, Decca Records made 3 double faced phonograph records with stories from Raggedy Ann and the Magic Book, Raggedy Ann and the Golden Butterfly and Raggedy Ann and Andy and the Nice Fat Policeman.

M5 Rag Doll's Adventures in Animal Land. (33rpm) Featuring a song titled, "Ragdoll Meets The Magic Mouse". Happy House Records #C-23. Manufactured by Hadden Record Corp. U.S.A. Album does not indicate year released. EV: $5-8

M10 Raggedy and Andy Pop Concert "The Raggedy Rollers" 33rpm album. Made by Kid Stuff Records #KSS137. 1976, 1978 & 1980 for The Bobbs-Merrill Company, Inc. EV: $8-10 "Have fun with Raggedy Ann and the Raggedy Rollers! Songs include: *Rock Around the Clock, Hound Dog, Splish Splash, Shake Rattle and Roll, Sha Boom,* and *My Girl Lollypop.*"

M6 Raggedy Ann and Andy "A Musical Adventure" An 87 minute color CBS/ FOX Video VHS # 7084. The first animated feature, the story is based on Johnny Gruelle's "Raggedy Ann and Andy and the Camel with the Wrinkled Knees". Macmillan, Inc 1977. *"America's favorite doll on a whirlwind journey through fantasyland."* Songs by Joe Raposo, a former Sesame Street songwriter. Also available in DVD. EV: $18-20

M24 Raggedy Ann and Andy's Alphabet Book and Record. SEE the pictures, HEAR the story, READ the book. Kid Stuff KSR625. 1980 The Bobbs-Merrill Company, Inc. EV: $12-15

M25 Raggedy Ann and Andy's Book of Manners Record and Book. SEE the pictures, HEAR the story, READ the book. Kid Stuff KSR 965. 1980 The Bobbs-Merrill Company, Inc. EV: $12-15

M27 Kids Klassics VHS # K1409. Contains four fully animated cartoons. Approximate playing time 30 minutes. Features: "The Enchanted Square" (color) and "Suddenly It's Spring" (B/W) both starring Raggedy Ann. Made 1985 New York. EV: $6-8

M29 Raggedy Ann and Andy, The Great Santa Caper VHS #6045. The award winning animation and sound track! Written, produced and directed by Chuck Jones. Approximately 30 minute color cartoon. Made by United American Video (UAV) in 1991 for Macmillan 1993. Raggedy Ann and Andy travel to the North Pole to save Christmas! EV: $12

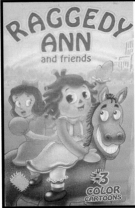

M28 Raggedy Ann and Friends VHS #3025. Three color cartoons. Approximate playing time 30 minutes. Made in 1988 by United American Video (UAV). EV: $6-8

♫ **DYK:** "Suddenly It's Spring" was originally made famous by Ginger Rogers in the film, "Lady In The Dark", 1941.

♫ **DYK:** A Christmas special is typically a one-time, 30 minute animated program aired during the Christmas season. Some are extended episodes of currently running television series featuring the regular characters. The Great Santa Caper was aired as a Christmas special in 1978, directed by Chuck Jones.

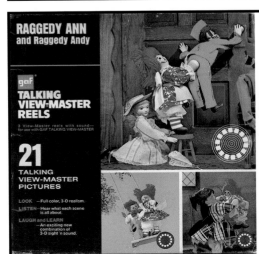

M36 Raggedy Ann and Andy Talking View Master Reels. 3 view master reels with sound-for use with GAF Talking View-Master. Twenty-one talking pictures, full color and 3-D realism. The talking version became available in 1973. Made by GAF Corporation. A non-talking model was released in 1971. Reel one: How Raggedy Ann Learns a Lesson. Reel two: Raggedy Andy Arrives. Reel three: Doctor Raggedy Andy. EV: $18-20

M37a Classic Raggedy Ann and Andy Treasures From the Heart CD Set. A collection of merry melodies for a day of fun! The three (40-50 minute each) CD set includes M37b "Classic Stories & Nursery Rhymes" M37c "Classic Children's Songs" and M37d "Spirit of America". The music line debuted in 2003 by San Diego based Genius Products and signed a multi-year licensing agreement with United Media, the licensing agent for Simon & Schuster and publisher of Raggedy Ann and Andy classic children's books. The CD's are sold individually and in multi-packs. RV: $12 for multi-pack, $5 for individual CD's.

M38a Raggedy Ann Stories CD. Listeners hear all the original Raggedy Ann stories first published in 1918 by Johnny Gruelle. Narrated by Cicely Tyson. Copyright 1993 by The Last Great Company recorded with permission from Simon & Schuster. M38b CD back. RV: $17.95

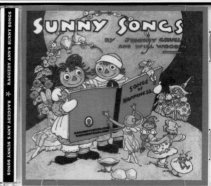 

M39a Sunny Songs CD. Digital version of the original recording by Radio Revisited. Children's songs with instrumental accompaniment. M39b CD close up. Original music written by Johnny Gruelle and Will Woodin. Vocals by Frank Luther. EV: $15

M40 Cartoon Craze presents *"Raggedy Ann (1941), Suddenly It's Spring"* (1944) DVD. 61 minutes color, 8 episodes including "The Enchanted Square (1947)". 2004 Digiview Productions, L.L.C. Made in Taiwan. www.digiviewus.com RV: $1.00 Can be found in discount stores.

M41 Raggedy Ann VHS #3337. Color, approximate running time 30 minutes. Printed in U.S.A. 1987 Star Classics Inc. Original cartoons produced in the 1930's and 1940's. EV: $6

M42 Kid Video presents Raggedy Ann VHS #10004. Classic cartoons in full color. The color-enhanced figure represented on the front of the box is taken directly from the actual public domain cartoon. 1989 HEP CAT Entertainment, Nashville, TN. Video label 1989 United American Video P.O. Box 7647 Charlotte, NC 28241. EV: $7

M43 Raggedy Ann and Other Cartoon Classics VHS PA-1007 Vol 1. "The Enchanted Square". 1994 Parents Approved Video. P.O. Box 630662 Ojus, FL 33163. The pictures on this package are taken directly from the actual public domain cartoon. EV: $6

M44 Raggedy Ann and Friends Funtime Kid VHS #3025. Approximate running time 30 minutes in color. Made in U.S.A. 1989 United American Video. Featuring "The Enchanted Square". EV: $6

M45 Raggedy Ann VHS #20018. Diamond Entertainment Corporation. Spanish version. 1990 Anaheim, CA. "El Cuadrado Eucatado" (The Enchanted Square) EV: $6

M46 Raggedy Ann Cartoon Favorites VHS #13007. Color & B/W approximate running time 30 minutes. Package designed and distributed by Trans-Atlantic Video S. Plainfield, NJ. 1980's. Featuring "The Enchanted Square". EV: $6

M47 Raggedy Ann Starring in *The Enchanted Square* (1947) plus two other cartoons VHS # 3025. FunTime Kid Video in color. Approximate running time 30 minutes. 1987 United American Video Corporation. EV: $6

M48 Raggedy Ann And Other Cartoon Classics VHS # 1007. Four fully animated color cartoons. 1992 Parents approved video. Featuring "The Enchanted Square (1947)". EV: $6

M50 Cartoon Carnival Raggedy Ann and Friends VHS # 3524. In color, approximate running time 120 minutes. 1985 United American Video Entertainment. Featuring "The Enchanted Square (1947)". EV: $7

M49 The Adventures of Raggedy Ann and Andy "The Magic Wings Adventure" VHS #8299. CBS /FOX Video 1988. Printed in U.S.A. Closed captioned. Approximate running time 30 minutes. Viewers are delighted by magic eggs and Trolitt the ugly troll! EV: $12

M51 The Adventures of Raggedy Ann and Andy "The Mabbit Adventure" VHS # 5960. Closed captioned, approximately 30 minutes. 1988 CBS/FOX Video. There's trouble in Mabbit Land! EV: $12

M52 The Adventures of Raggedy Ann and Andy "The Little Chicken Adventure" VHS #8298. HiFi Stereo closed captioned. 1988 CBS Inc. Printed in U. S. A. Running time 30 minutes. Viewers are enchanted by the Raggedy's, Little Chicken and Great White who outsmart the rustlers! EV: $12

M53 The Adventures of Raggedy Ann and Andy "The Ransom of Sunny Bunny" VHS #5961. HiFi Stereo CBS/Fox Video 1988. Cracklen the Wizard, Mynx the Witch and Raggedy Dog entertain viewers. EV: $12

M54 Raggedy Ann and Friends Kid Flicks VHS #2015. Fully animated color cartoons, running time 31 minutes. 1985 Interglobal Home Video. Toronto, Canada. EV: $6

M55 Raggedy Ann and Andy "The Pumpkin Who Couldn't Smile" VHS # 5883. Award winning animation and super soundtrack! United American Video Corporation. 1993 Macmillan, Inc. Running time 30 minutes. Written, produced and directed by Chuck Jones. Ann and Andy save Ralph's Halloween! This was a Halloween television special directed by Chuck Jones in 1979. EV: $12

M56 The Adventures of Raggedy Ann and Andy "The Christmas Adventure" VHS # 8150. Color, approximately 25 minutes. 1988 CBS, Inc. Someone has stolen Santa's reindeer, sleigh and all the toys! EV: $12

M57 The Adventures of Raggedy Ann and Andy "The Pirate Adventure" VHS # 5959. CBS/FOX Video 1998. Approximately 30 minutes. Viewers are delighted by a story of Fido, a Leprechaun and a treasure map! EV: $12

M58 Cartoon Classics Raggedy Ann and Friends VHS # 83205. Color, approximately 26 minutes. 1991 Alpha Video Distributors, Inc. Featuring "The Enchanted Square (1947)" EV: $6-8

M59 The Snowden Raggedy Ann and Andy Holiday Show VHS #58190034. 1998 Snowden Smith-Hemion /Target Stores production. Length 60 minutes. Starring Scott Hamilton. Includes exciting footage of the making of the show. EV: $12-15

♫ **DYK:** CBS featured a TV special titled "Snowden on Ice", aired on November 27, 1998.
www.gordeeva.com

M102 Snowden Raggedy Ann & Andy's Adventure VHS Approximately 23 minutes, color 1998. Peyton Hudson Corporation is the author of the motion picture for the purpose of copyright and other laws. EV: $10-12

M92 Raggedy Ann and Andy A Musical Adventure VHS. Released 1977 by MacMillan, Inc. and Playhouse Video. Songs by Joe Raposo. An animated children's adventure with the two famous dolls as its stars. EV: $10-12

M80a Raggedy Ann and Andy Happiness Album. Kid Stuff Phono Picture Disc. 33rpm record. Limited Edition Collector Series KPD 6001. 1981 The Bobbs-Merrill Company, Inc. Produced by John Braden. Distributed by I. J. E. Distributing, Hollywood FL. M80b Album close up. Songs include *Raggedy Ann World, Suppose, Brother, Come and Dance With Me, Happy Is, This Old Man* and *Raggedy Ann and Andy World (reprise)*. EV: $8-12

M86a Raggedy Ann and Andy Christmas party album. Kid Stuff Records KSS # 5006. 1976, 1978, 1980 The Bobbs-Merrill Company, Inc. Distributed by IJE Distributing, Inc. Hollywood, FL. Raggedy Ann and Andy Christmas Party Holiday Dreams Come True as Raggedy Ann and Andy Visit Santa for a Christmas Eve Party. M86b Inside album. Story and songs; *Jingle Bells, We Wish You A Merry Christmas, Silver Bells, Santa Claus is Coming to Town, The Night Before Christmas*. EV: $8-10

M62 True Value Hardware Stores Happy Holiday 33 rpm record. Cover features a handmade Raggedy Ann. RCA Special Products Vol 19. 1984 RCA Records by RCA Corporation New York, New York. Features Julie Andrews, The Carpenters and Bing Crosby. EV: $6-8

M99a,b Duo-Art Piano Roll #19685. Raggedy Ann The Stepping Stones. Song piano roll with words played by Frank Banta. M99b close up 1923 EV: $6-8

♪ **DYK:** A Raggedy Ann and Andy Book & Tape set sold at Wal-Mart in 1999. Retail price was $3.96. It is the complete story of The Pumpkin Who Couldn't Smile. Book is paperback, recorded on cassette tape.

M103a Raggedy Ann and Andy Meet Dizzy Izzy and The Witch a 45rpm, 1974 Bobbs-Merrill Co. for Hallmark. M103b Read along pop-up story record with theme song. M103c Close up. EV: $5-7

M109 Raggedy Ann & Andy Christmas Party Cassette. A complete LP Record on this tape. Kid Stuff Records # KST 4006 distributed by I. J. E. Distributing. 1976, 1978, 1980 The Bobbs-Merrill Company, Inc. EV: $8-10

♪ **DYK:** Hallmark also made other read-a-long pop up books for The Bobbs-Merrill Company, Inc. Titles: Raggedy Ann and Andy in Dreamland, Raggedy Ann and Andy on a Journey Beneath the Enchanted Pond, and Raggedy Ann and Andy Visit the Kingdom of "Every Wish".

M117a Raggedy Ann and Andy on a Trip To The Stars 45 rpm, read-a-long story record...with theme song! 1974 The Bobbs-Merrill Co., Inc for Hallmark. M117b Open the record to reveal pop up photos of Andy, Henny the little Dutch doll and Ann baking cookies. EV: $5

M181a Raggedy Ann and Andy Go To Cookie Town 45 rpm, read-a-long story record...with theme song! 1974 The Bobbs-Merrill Company, Inc for Hallmark. M181b Open the book to reveal pop up photos of Ann, Andy and all their friends visiting with sweety-tooth dragon in Cookie Town. EV: $5

M114a The Adventures of Raggedy Ann and Andy The Perriwonk Adventure. Color VHS 1988 CBS Inc. Approximately 30 minutes. M114b Back "Raggedy Andy runs off with Marcella's gold bracelet" EV: $12

Raggedy Ann & Andy
AT THE CIRCUS

This is your Raggedy Ann and Andy Read-a-long book. Every time you hear this chime....it means you are to turn the page in your storybook. Now we are ready to begin our adventure into the Land of Fun. Open your book and we will start the story of RAGGEDY ANN AND ANDY AT THE CIRCUS. Remember, when you hear the chime, turn the page.

M112a Raggedy Ann & Andy at the Circus Read-a-long book and record. SEE the pictures HEAR the story READ the book. Kid Stuff Records KSR 966 Distributed by I. J. E. Distributing, Hollywood Florida. 1980 The Bobbs-Merrill Company, Inc. M112b Page one of book, "When you hear the chime, turn the page!" EV: $5

M123a Raggedy Ann and Andy's Alphabet & Numbers LP. "An Introduction to the Alphabet & Numbers with Raggedy Ann & Andy proves learning can be fun." Kid Stuff Records. Copyright 1976, 1978, 1980 The Bobbs-Merrill Company, Inc. Distribution by Disque Kid Stuff, Montee de Liesse, Montreal M123b Back cover. EV: $8-10

M131a Adventures of Raggedy Ann and Andy cel. Episode 4, Scene 219A/C7 entitled Beastly Ghost. M131b CBS Entertainment Certificate of Authenticity through an exclusive arrangement with The Michael Bandy Company. CBS Inc. 1990. The names and depictions of Raggedy Ann, Raggedy Andy and all associated characters are trademarks of MacMillan, Inc. EV: $25-30

M130a Adventures of Raggedy Ann and Andy cel. Episode 4, Scene 27/G10 entitled Beastly Ghost. M130b CBS Entertainment Certificate of Authenticity through an exclusive arrangement with The Michael Bandy Company. CBS Inc. 1990. The names and depictions of Raggedy Ann, Raggedy Andy and all associated characters are trademarks of MacMillan, Inc. EV: $25-35

♫ **DYK:** The Adventures of Raggedy Ann and Andy cartoon was a Saturday morning favorite making their debut at the time of their 70th anniversary in 1988, running from 9/17/88-9/07/91 on CBS. Raggedy Ann and Andy and their nursery friends were stuffed dolls that had adventures. The dolls destination of choice was a place called Raggedyland. The cast included Raggedy Ann, Raggedy Andy, Raggedy Cat, Raggedy Dog, Grouchy Bear, Sunny Bunny, The Camel with the Wrinkled Knees, and Marcella. www.yesterdayland.com & www.80scartoons.net

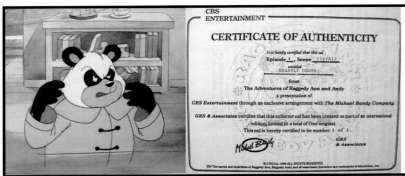

M132a Adventures of Raggedy Ann and Andy cel. Episode 4, Scene 116/A12 entitled Beastly Ghost. M132b CBS Entertainment Certificate of Authenticity through an exclusive arrangement with The Michael Bandy Company. CBS Inc. 1990. The names and depictions of Raggedy Ann, Raggedy Andy and all associated characters are trademarks of MacMillan, Inc. EV:$25-30

M137a Songs of Raggedy Ann and Andy. 1948 RCA Victor Youth Series. Two record set 78 rpm. Johnny Gruelle Co. Color the figures with crayons. Jack Arthur with Paul Taubman & Orchestra. Lyrics by Johnny Gruelle. Music by Will Woodin and Charles Miller. M137b Back cover. EV: $25-35

M140 Little Jimmy Dickens 45rpm with side one (You've been quite doll) "Raggedy Ann". EV: $2-4

♪ DYK: Little Jimmy Dickens was 4'11, known as "Tater" and was a regular on the Grand Ole Opry! The song, *"Raggedy Ann (You've Been Quite a Doll)"* written by Red Lane is a tearful recitation of a grieving man's talk with the treasured doll that guards his daughter's grave. This was one of most requested numbers performed by Little Jimmie Dickens.

M141a Raggedy Ann & Andy Bend and Stretch Record. A very Special Exercise Record for Children. "Who says exercise can't be fun? Raggedy Ann & Andy have found the perfect way to help your children stay in shape with this fun-filled album of exercises, songs and creative dance." M141b Back cover: Introduce your children to Raggedy Ann & Andy and open up a whole new world of fitness & fun for the entire family. Kid Stuff Records. Distributed by IJE Distributing, Inc. Hollywood, FL 1976, 1978, 1980 The Bobbs-Merrill Company, Inc. EV: $6-8

M149a Raggedy Ann & Andy's Dance Party 33LP. Songs: Bunny Hop, The Twist, Comin' Round the Mountain, Disco, Disco, Que Sera, and Hokey Pokey. By Kid Stuff Records KSS 160. 1976, 1978, 1980. The Bobbs-Merrill Company, Inc. M149b Back cover. EV: $8-10

SONG BOOK

This is your Raggedy Ann and Andy Sing Along Book. Read along and learn the words and then we will sing the songs. Every time you hear this chime ... it means that you are to turn the page in your song book. Now we are ready to begin our adventure into the Land of Songs. Open your Raggedy Ann and Andy Song Book and we will begin. Remember, when you hear the chime turn the page.

M147a Raggedy Ann & Andy's Song Book. Listen to the words AND then Sing-a-long. 1980 The Bobbs-Merrill Company, Inc. M147b,c book artwork. Based on the characters created by Johnny Gruelle. Kid Stuff Records. Distributed by I. J. E. Distributing Hollywood, FL EV: $4-6

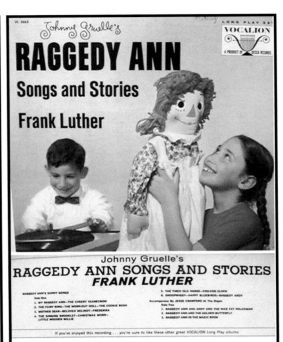

M150a Johnny Gruelle's Raggedy Ann Songs and Stories Frank Luther Long Play 33 1/3 VL 3665. 1960's. Vocalion A product of Decca Records. M150b Back cover. Copyright 1939-1940-1942 by The Johnny Gruelle Company. Original price $2.99. EV: $8-10 Side One: *My Raggedy Ann, The Cheery Scarecrow, The Fairy Ring, The Worn-Out Doll, The Cookie Bush, Mother Dear, Beloved Belindy, Fredericka, The Singing Brooklet, Christmas Morn, Little Wooden Willie, The Tired Old Horse, Coo Coo Clock, Snoopwiggy, Happy Bluebirds, Raggedy Andy.* Side two: *Raggedy Ann and Andy and the Nice Fat Policeman, Raggedy Ann and The Golden Butterfly, Raggedy Ann In the Magic Book.*

M146a Raggedy Ann & Andy Christmas Fun Book & rpm record. SEE the pictures, HEAR the story, READ the book. 1980 The Bobbs-Merrill Company, Inc. M146b Back cover. M146c Inside view. Based on the characters created by Johnny Gruelle. Kid Stuff Records. Distributed by I. J. E. Distributing Hollywood, FL EV: $4-6

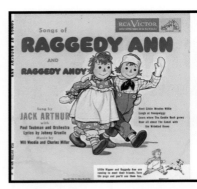

M162 *"Songs of Raggedy Ann & Andy"* RCA Victor Little Nipper series. 45 rpm 2-record set. Sung by Jack Arthur with Paul Taubman and Orchestra. Lyrics by Johnny Gruelle. Music by Will Woodin and Charles Miller. Copyright 1949 The Johnny Gruelle Co. The set sleeve is a four page song/story book. EV: EC $25 GC $18-20

♪ **DYK:** The "Leave It to Beaver" TV show's theme song was based upon a children's tune called *"The Toy Parade,"* written by Melvyn Leonard. The lyrics include mention of Raggedy Ann! www.leaveittobeaver.org

Stories available on cassette from www.recordedbooks.com & www.audible.com

1. *Raggedy Ann & Andy Leaf Dance*, unabridged cassette written by Bobby Pearlman, narrated by Christina Moore.

2. *Raggedy Ann & Andy: Going to Grandma's*, unabridged cassette written by Patricia Hall, narrated by Christina Moore.

3. *Raggedy Ann & Andy: School Day Adventure*, unabridged cassette written by Patricia Hall, narrated by Christina Moore.

4. *Raggedy Ann and Andy: Day at the Fair*, unabridged cassette written by Patricia Hall, narrated by Christina Moore.

5. *Raggedy Ann Stories & Raggedy Andy Stories*, unabridged audio book, 1996. Written by Johnny Gruelle, narrated by Kristine Underwood.

SHEET MUSIC & SONGBOOKS

Close up of Johnny Gruelle's drawing on the cover of Raggedy Ann's Sunny Songs song book.

M7 The Stepping Stones with Dorothy Stone, "In Love With Love" sheet music by Anne Caldwell and Jerome Kern. 1923. The cover art is a duplicate of Johnny Gruelle's Raggedy Andy Stories. EV: $15-20

♫ **DYK:** Jerome Kern's 1923 fox trot "Raggedy Ann" was composed for the 1923 stage musical "The Stepping Stones" and is on Wurlitzer 165 Roll No. 6624. You can hear the tune played on the Seabreeze band organ at http://wurlitzer-rolls.com/sounds.html

M63a The Stepping Stones with Dorothy Stone. "Raggedy Ann" sheet music. Words by Anne Caldwell. Music by Jerome Kern. MCMXXII (1922) T. B. Harms Co. New York. Six sheet music booklets were published; *Everybody Calls Me Little Red Riding Hood, In Love With Love, Once in a Blue Moon, One Lovely Rose Pie, Raggedy Ann and Wonderful Dad.* EV: $12-15
M63b A matching Raggedy Ann tote bag EV: 25.00

♫ **DYK:** Do you have trouble converting roman numerals to numbers? Here is a web site that will convert a number to roman numeral or vice versa. http://www.novaroma.org/via_romana/numbers.html

M61a Raggedy Ann's Sunny Songs Book. Words and drawings by Johnny Gruelle. Music by Will Woodin. Copyright 1930 by Miller Music, Inc. Printed in U.S.A. New York. Publisher- EMI Miller Publishing, NY. Inside cover; *"To little children everywhere this book is lovingly dedicated."* M61b The Fairy Ring music and lyrics. Also printed as hard cover edition. M61c Back cover. EV: $25-30

M64a Song Hits. *"A Legally Authorized Lyric Magazine".* April 1941. M64b page 11 has lyrics of the song *"Raggedy Ann".* (From the Paramount Production "Raggedy Ann" [and Raggedy Andy]") and *"You're A Calico Millionaire".* By Dave Fleischer and Sammy Timberg. Copyright 1941 by Famous Music Corp. Original cost of the magazine 10 cents.

M65 Raggedy Song Book. All original music and lyrics by Susan Ann Garrison. Inspired by characters from Raggedy Ann Children's books by Johnny B. Gruelle. Copyright 2001. Book contains sheet music for 8 songs. EV: $12-15

M66 The Stepping Stones with Dorothy Stone. "Everybody Call Me Little Red Riding Hood" sheet music. Words by Anne Caldwell. Music by Jerome Kern. MCMXXII (1922) T. B. Harms Co. EV: $10-12

M94 Raggedy Ann Joyful Songs Book. Illustrated and written by Johnny Gruelle. 48 pages with 12 full page illustrations. 20 songs with music for the piano, plus many original illustrations. It measures 8" by 11". Music by Chas Miller Published 1937 by Miller Music Corporation, NY 1937. EV: $25-28 The songs titles are: *Magic Songs of Happiness, Wishing Song, Pop-Corn Clouds, Potatoes, The Giant, Little Bertha Bumble Bee, How Do the Flowers Know the Way?, The Sky, The Looking-Glass Brook, Hoppy Toad, The Hootie Owls, Sailing On, Why Should I Not Be Happy?, Leaden Soldiers, Johnny Cricket, Little Pig, The Funny Old Crows, The Camel With the Wrinkled Knees, Wallie Woodpecker and Song of Darkness*

M128a Song Hits magazine. Volume 4, No. 10 March 1941. M128b page 10 features the words to the *"Raggedy Ann"* song written by Al J. Nelburg, Dave Fleischer and Sammy Timberg. Copyright 1941.

M129 Toy Shop Frolics sheet music piano solo by William Scher. Boston Music Co. 1980's. Cover features Raggedy Ann and Raggedy Andy. EV: $5-7

43

♫

MUSIC WORKS

A bus full of Raggedys heading to Arcola! Can you hear them singing,
"The Wheels on the Bus Go Round and Round?"

Songs with titles like: "Raggedy Ann," "Raggedy Anne," "Raggedy Andy"

Sources: www.allmusic.com, www.ascap.com, http://repertoire.bmi.com

Song Title	Composer/ Writer	Performing Artist	Album Title	Year	Genre
"Raggedy Ann (You've Been Quite a Doll)"	Red Lane	Little Jimmie Dickens	*From the Vaults: Decca Classics*	1994	Vocal
"Raggedy Ann (You've Been Quite a Doll)"	De Laughter	Little Jimmie Dickens	*I'm Little But I'm Loud: the Little Jimmie Dickens Collection*	1996	Country
"Raggedy Ann and Me" (2:06)	Browne	Severin Browne	*Severin Browne*	1973	Rock
"Ragtime Raggedy Ann" (2:21)	Gibson	Harry Gibson	*Everybody's Crazy But Me*	1986	Rock/ Swing/ Jive
"Raggedy Ann and Player Piano" (2:21)	Lewis/ Smith	Margaret Lewis	*Lonesome Bluebird*	1995	Swamp Pop
"Raggedy Andy" (5:17)	Unknown	Katie's Dimples	*Come With*	1995	Rock/ Alt Pop/Rock
"Raggedy Anne" (2:17)	Unknown	Jimmy Bowen	*Best of Jimmy Bowen*	1991	Rock & Roll / Rockabilly
"You're Not Charlie Brown (And I'm Not Raggedy Ann)"	Unknown	Donna Fargo	*The Best of Donna Fargo*	1995	Country
"Raggedy Ann"	Henske	Craig Doerge	*Craig Dorege*		Rock
"Raggedy Ann" (3:00)	Jarreau	Al Jarreau	*We Got By* www.aljarreau.com	1975 & 1988	Jazz
"Raggedy Ann" (2:53)	Public domain	Benton Flippen	*Old Time, New Times*	1994	Blues
"Raggedy Ann"	Knox/Bowen	Buddy Knox, Jimmy Bowen & The Rhythm Orchids	*The Complete Roulette Recordings*	1996	Rockabilly
"Raggedy Ann"	Evans/ Hughes	Buddy Knox	*The Complete Roulette Recordings*	1975	Rock/ Rockabilly
"Raggedy Ann" (2:53)	Caldwell/ Kern	Andrea Marcovicci	*Just Kern*	1992	Vocal/ Traditional Pop
"Raggedy Ann" (6:49)	Lee Morgan	Lee Morgan	*Jazz Trumpet, Vol 1: Classic Jazz to Swing*	1983	Jazz/ Swing

Song Title	Composer/ Writer	Performing Artist	Album Title	Year	Genre
"Raggedy Ann" (6:46)	Lee Morgan	Lee Morgan	Take Twelve	1962	Jazz /Hard Bop
"Raggedy Ann" (2:42)	Judy Reynolds	Judy Reynolds	Rockin' on Broadway: The Time, Brent, Shad Story	2000	Rock & Roll, Pop/Rock
"Raggedy Ann" (2:37)	Owens	Charlie Rich	The Fabulous Charlie Rich	1969	Country
"Raggedy Ann" (2:24)	Marr	John Randolph Marr	John Randolph Marr		Rock
"Raggedy Ann"	Mindy Smith	Mindy Smith	One Moment More	2004	Country
"Raggedy Ann and Andy"	Music and lyrics Joe Raposo	unknown	Produced 1985 as Rag Dolly Produced 1986 as Raggedy Ann	1984	unknown

Musical Works written by Johnny Gruelle per ASCAPI @ *www.ascap.com*

"Beloved Belindy"

"Camel with the Wrinkled Knees"

"Cheery Scarecrow"

"Christmas Morn"

"The Coo Coo Clock"

"Cookie Bush"

"Could I Have Every Wish Come True"

"Fairy Ring"

"Fredericka"

"Happy Bluebirds"

"How Do Flowers Know"

"Little Bertha Bumblebee"

"Little Wooden Willie"

"Magic Hearts of Candy FR RA"

"Magic Songs of Happiness"

"My Raggedy Ann"

"Popcorn Clouds"

"Potatoes"

"Raggedy Andy"

"Raggedy Ann Sunny Songs"

"Singing Brooklet"

"Tired Old Horse"

"Wishing Song"

"Worn Out Doll"

♪

RAGGEDY ANN BOOKS

(with special magical musical moments)

Raggedy Ann always played the piano.

Johnny Gruelle illustration, "Raggedy Ann always played the piano",
from the story Raggedy Ann and Maizie Moocow,
Raggedy Ann & Andy's Merry Adventures.

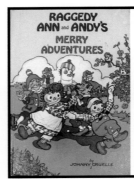

M155a,b "Raggedy Ann and Andy's Merry Adventures" written and illustrated by Johnny Gruelle. The Bobbs-Merrill Company Inc. 1974.

"After everyone had enjoyed about leventy-leven dishes of ice cream and had eaten ninety-ninety ladyfinger cookies, Mrs. Moocow asked Raggedy Ann to play the piano. The Raggedys had visited Mrs. Moocow many times, and Raggedy Ann always played the piano. Raggedy Ann knew only one tune, "Peter, Peter, Pumpkin Eater," and she used only two notes at a time, for she played with her rag thumbs, but it was a very, very tinkly tuney. So Raggedy Ann tinkled the Moocow piano with her two rag thumbs, and it sounded so lovely that everyone grew hungry and Maizie Moocow and Raggedy Andy had to serve three more dishes of ice cream to everyone. Then, after Raggedy Ann had washed the ice cream from around Raggedy Andy's painted smile, everyone had a nice surprise, for Betty Abbott sat down at the Moocow piano and played "Home Sweet Home" and "Way Down Upon the Suwannee River." Betty had taken lessons and could play the piano with her two thumbs and all eight of her other fingers."

M87 "Raggedy Andy Stories" written and illustrated by Johnny Gruelle. This book introduces the little rag brother of Raggedy Ann. 1960 The Bobbs-Merrill Company, Inc. Original copyright 1920 P. F. Volland Co. renewed 1947 by Myrtle Gruelle and in 1948 by The Johnny Gruelle Company.

Henny, the Dutch doll, dragged the little square music box out into the center of the room and wound it up. Then all, catching hands, danced in a circle around it, laughing and shouting in their tiny doll voices.

"I will tell you the secret of my singing, "said the shell. " When anyone puts his ear to me and listens, he hears the reflection of his own heart's music, singing; so, you see, while I say that I am singing all the time, in reality I sing only when someone full of happiness hears his own singing as if it were mine."

M93 "Raggedy Ann in the Deep Deep Woods" written and illustrated by Johnny Gruelle. The Bobbs-Merrill Company, Inc. 1960.

"So after, the picnic, the deep woods, filled with fairies 'n' everything rang with the songs and merry chatter of the happy little woodland creatures."

"Ten little fairies played there, and their tiny voices sounded as sweet, as they sang in their game, as the wind when it plays upon an Aeolian harp."

"Raggedy Ann wishes for a real for sure organ for Gran'ma and Gran'pa Hootie Owl that could squeak out beautiful tunes for anyone that know how to play it. "

"With so much to see when strolling through the woods and with the music of the birds happy in their tree swings, I do not see how anyone can help but feel his whole soul filled with the sunshine of happiness."

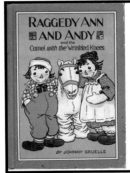

M105 "Raggedy Ann and Andy and the Camel with the Wrinkled Knees" written and illustrated by Johnny Gruelle 1960 The Bobbs-Merrill Company, Inc. Copyright 1924 by John B. Gruelle. Copyright renewed 1951 by Myrtle Gruelle. Copyright 1951 by the Johnny Gruelle Company. Copyright Great Britain, 1924 and 1951.

From the outside came the songs of the little creatures who live in the grasses and the flowers and above these sounds Raggedy Ann and Raggedy Andy heard the "Squeek! Squeek! Squeekity-squeek!" of Johnny Cricket's fiddle as Johnny bounced up and down upon his seat on a tall blade of grass."

M107 "Beloved Belindy" written and illustrated by Johnny Gruelle.1960 The Bobbs-Merrill Company, Inc. Copyright 1926 The P. F. Volland Co. Copyright 1941 by Myrtle Gruelle. Copyright renewed 1953 by Myrtle Gruelle.

Beloved Belindy held up her rag hand and, when the dolls became quiet, she said, "We have a toy piano, so that will do for the music you always find in an amusement park."

M159a Raggedy Ann and Andy comic by Johnny Gruelle. A Dell Magazine. Volume 1 No 16, September 1947. Published monthly by Dell Publishing Company, Inc. M159b In this issue "Bertram Bear sings a tune." Each issue contained a Raggedy Ann cartoon story, an animal picture story, an Animal Mother Goose section, the Raggedy's Good Manners feature "The Raggedy Way" M159c, a fairy tale, illustrated poems, a color up page, a Billy and Bonny Bee cartoon story, and animal photographs. With the exception of the fairy tale, each story was new, original and illustrated with a multitude of delightful pictures. Printed in USA. Original cost 10 cents each. A yearly subscription was $1.00 or $1.75 for two years. EV: $20-25

M168a Raggedy Ann's Sweet and Dandy, Sugar Candy Scratch and Sniff Book by Patricai Thackray, pictures by Carol Nicklaus. A Golden Scratch and Sniff Book by Golden Press New York 1976 The Bobbs-Merrill Company, Inc. M168b *The Raggedys celebrated Little Raisin's homecoming by playing and singing a favorite ol song, "Love's Return".*

M191a, b, c Raggedy Ann and Andy's Grow-and-Learn Library. 1988 Macmillan, Inc. Lynx Books. Volume 5, "What Can A Camel Do?"

While The Camel sat and thought, he listened to Raggedy Ann play "Twinkle, Twinkle, Little Star" on Marcella's toy piano, Ping, ping, Ping, ping, Ping, Ping, ping. The notes rang out loud and clear. And Raggedy Dog and Raggedy Cat sand the words. "Now that's an idea," The Camel said happily. "If Raggedy Dog and Raggedy Cat can sing, perhaps I can, too."

M192a, b, c Raggedy Ann & Andy's Grow-and-Learn Library. 1988 Macmillan, Inc. Lynx Books. Volume 11, "The Jack-In-The-Box."

"Do you think you'd like a little music for your circus?" Jack Asked. He reached over to crank the handle on the side of his box. "What perfect circus music!" said The Camel. Jack kept turning the handle.

M193a,b,c Raggedy Ann & Andy's Grow-and-Learn Library. 1988 Macmillan, Inc. Lynx Books. Volume 17, "The Birthday Surprise"

"How about a drum?" suggested Tim the Toy Soldier. "Maybe we could make a drum for him. That would be a great surprise!" "No, no---I have a better idea!" shouted Greta the Dutch Doll. "Maybe we could practice a Dutch song, and The Camel could dance to it when he gets home."

INTERNET RESOURCES

About.com — A Raggedy search results in Web links, articles, collector's photos, and the Johnny Gruelle Fairy Art gallery.

angelwinks.webby.com — Delight your friends by sending them a free online postcard. Scroll down and click on Raggedy Ann & Andy Card Shoppe. Six to choose from!

amazon.com — Retail site. Do a Raggedy search—find gifts, books, videos, toys...and links to online shops and auctions.

applause.com — As of October 2004, RUSS Berry & Co., Inc. added Applause to its family of brands. Click on Applause and scroll down to "RUSS Becomes Master License For Raggedy Ann and Andy" news release. Check this site for new products.

Arcolachamber.com — Information about the annual Raggedy Ann festival in Illinois.

Birthdayexpress.com — Raggedy Ann cake recipe and party supplies.

cherylmelody.com — A fun children's music site.

childrensbooksonline.com — Raggedy Ann Alphabet book.

cynthianaky.com — Search for news releases about the annual Raggedy Ann festival in Kentucky.

collectorsparadise.com — Retail site.

coloring.ws/raggedy1.htm — Raggedy Ann and Andy-themed coloring pages.

countryfair.com — (RAGTIME Dollies booth #125) The place to buy and sell Raggedy crafts on the Internet. Electronic virtual booths!

dogpile.com — Do Raggedy search for lots of Web site and retail sources.

dollcradle.com — Offers a variety of Raggedy Ann merchandise.

Dltk-teach.com/books/raggedy/puzzle1.htm — Raggedy Ann online jigsaw puzzle.

drtoy.com — Toy history timeline.

ebay.com — An auction house with loads of Raggedy stuff!

funtocollect.com — Retail dolls, books, and Enesco figurines.

Harpergeneralstore.com — The Raggedy Ann corner is a fun place to visit.

hobbdolls.com — Hobbs House of Dolls. John Gruelle history and retail available.

judyanddavid.com — The Children's Music Archives.

jwpepper.com — Pepper Music Network. Raggedy Ann and Andy (Gould, R.) Choral UNIS/2-PT... Grade-3.Leslie Music Supply $1.50.

kididdles.com — Musical "Mouseum" with kids' song lyrics.

kidzmusic.com — Site dedicated to children's music.

catalog.loc.gov — Library of Congress online catalog – search for songwriters.

mydeardolly.com — Search cloth doll and theme Raggedy Ann for formerly owned merchandise, commercial and handmade items.

nadda.org — (National Antique Doll Dealers Association). Electronic newsletter and show schedule.

niehs.nih.gov/kids/musicchildren.htm — The National Institute of Environmental Health Services— lyrics and music for many children's songs.

nytimes.com — Search for historical Raggedy articles.

pattyhall.com — A renowned Johnny Gruelle expert, folklorist, musician, and writer.

raggedyann.cc and **raggedys.com** — The Raggedys & Teddys retail site.

raggedyandrew.com — Andrew Tabbat's Web site.

raggedybook.com — A collector and author, Susan Ann Garrison's Web site.

raggedyman.com — The Last Great Company of Kim Gruelle.

raggedyann-museum.org — The official site for the Johnny Gruelle Raggedy Ann and Andy Museum. Arcola Illinois is the birthplace of Johnny Gruelle and the location of the official museum which opened in May 1999. Visit the Web, sign the guestbook, and check out the gift shop. The Arcola community annually celebrates a Raggedy Ann and Andy Festival each year.

raggedy-ann.com or **raggedyland.com** — This is the Raggedy Land gift shop, owned by Charles and Cheryl Platt. Voted in the TOP 10 of Doll Sites! Check out the What's New and Coming Soon pages!

raggedyplace.com — Online shopping catalog. Join the mailing list for new product releases and sales.

raggedysmiles.com — Primitive doll collections and patterns.

raggedyworld.com — Specialty Raggedy items sold only in Japan.

rankinpublishing.com or **ragsmag.com** — Subscribe to the *RAGS* magazine published quarterly.

simonsays.com — Simon and Schuster, Inc.

theraggedycottage.com — Vintage Raggedy treasures.

theraggedyspirit.com — Author's web site.

theriaults.com — World's leader in the auction of antique dolls.

theschoolbell.com — Great site for children's music!

trinachow.com — A Raggedy collector web site.

ufdc.org — (United Federation of Doll Clubs) A nonprofit organization with the goal of being the foremost in research, education, conservation, collecting, and appreciation of dolls. Check calendar for events near you and links to other doll-related sites.

unitedmedialicensing.com — Click on Brands for the latest information on licensing of Raggedy Ann products.

wurlitzer-rolls.com — Raggedy Ann (Fox Trot), from "The Stepping Stones" played by Vincent McKee © 1923 T. B. Harms Co. 0614 Standard "Play-a-roll" (with words) Standard Music rolls, South Orange, New Jersey. You can hear the tune played on the Seabreeze band organ on this Web site: **http://wurlitzer-rolls.com/sounds.html**.

COLLECTOR GUIDES

♫ Avery, Kim. *The World of Raggedy Ann Collectibles: Identification and Values.* Paducah, KY: Collector Books, 1997.

♫ Garrison, Susan Ann. *The Raggedy Ann and Andy Family Album.* Atglen, PA: Schiffer Publishing, 1989.

♫ Garrison, Susan Ann. *The Raggedy Ann & Andy Album, A Guide for Collectors. Third Edition.* Atglen, PA: Schiffer Publishing, 2000.

♫ Hall, Patricia. *Johnny Gruelle's Dolls and Merchandise.* Gretna, LA: Pelican Publishing, 2000.

♫ Lindenberger, Jan. *Raggedy Ann & Andy Collectibles, A Handbook and Price Guide.* Atglen, PA: Schiffer Publishing, 1995.

♫ Rhinehart, Joyce. *Wonderful Raggedy Anns.* Atglen, PA: Schiffer Publishing, 1997.

♫ Tabbat, Andrew. *The Collector's World of Raggedy Ann and Andy, Vol. 1.* Annapolis, MD: Gold Horse Publishing, 1996.

♫ Tabbat, Andrew. *The Collector's World of Raggedy Ann and Andy, Vol. 2.* Annapolis, MD: Gold Horse Publishing, 1997.

"MY RAGGEDY STORY"

My very first childhood memory of Raggedy Ann takes me back to the 1950's. My mother and I were embarking on a trip to Europe on the S.S. *United States* to join my father, an army pilot, who was stationed in Germany. I remember clutching the soft and cuddly cloth doll close to me as we boarded the large passenger ship. At three years old, I couldn't quite say the words, "Raggedy Ann," and was often heard saying, "love rags." Hence she became known as "Luvrags."

Together we explored the ship, climbing the grand staircase and strolling around the huge deck. I remember stuffing "Luvrags" inside my lifejacket during a lifeboat drill, because she was so scared. One evening, we peeked through the glass doors of the Grand Ballroom, listened to the orchestra playing, and watched as couples glided around the dance floor. Later, I learned that my mother had danced with Cary Grant that night!

In Kaiserslautern, Germany, we lived on the second floor of an apartment building. One autumn afternoon, Luvrags and I were watching my mother sewing us matching dresses. The window was open to let the cool fall air in, the leaves were blowing around on the ground and swirling high in the air as if they were dancing. I set Luvrags on the windowsill to watch, and suddenly the wind caught her and she flew out the window. We quickly ran down the stairs to the front lawn, but she was nowhere to be found. We asked the neighbors and the children playing nearby. No one had seen her fall from the window. She was gone.

To console me, my mother told me a story about how Luvrags had gone on an adventure to the Swiss Alps. She assured me that Luvrags would return to me someday. Whenever I asked if she was coming home today, she would comfort me with another tale of her adventures. My Mother tried very hard to find a replacement, but Raggedy Ann dolls were not available in Germany. By the time we returned to the United States fashion dolls like Barbie were all the rage and Raggedy Ann faded in my memories.

Many years later while walking through a flea market, I spotted something familiar. As I approached to get a better look, my heart started pounding. I picked up the faded rag doll and gently touched her dirty face and black button eyes. I was overcome with happiness and quickly recalled the soft warm comforting feelings that she had given me as a child.

"Luvrags" had finally returned to me, just as my mother had promised. Maybe someday, she will tell me about her windy ride on those fanciful magical leaves to the Swiss Alps and her long journey back to me in the United States.

Georgene 15" Raggedy Ann. (Luvrags) 1946-1963. Orange cotton yarn hair, four eyelashes and black button eyes. One sided tag on torso reads, "Johnny Gruelle's Own Raggedy Ann & Andy Dolls. Copyright P.F. Volland Co. 1918, 1920 Copyright Renewed Myrtle T. Gruelle, 1945, 1947. Georgene Novelties, Inc. New York City. Exclusive Licensed Manufacturer Made in U.S. A. " EV: $85-100

ORGANIZING YOUR COLLECTIBLES

Is your Raggedy Ann collection organized? Do you know how many items you have, what each item is worth, the manufacturer or what year it was made? Can you recall where you bought it or what you paid for it? Have you ever purchased an item only to discover it was a duplicate? If you are like me (crazy about Ann and Andy), you are always on the look out for anything Raggedy and can rarely resist buying more. My collection has grown so big over the past twenty eight years that I lost track of what I had and was struggling with all the above questions. I began researching organizational methods, gathering advice from various sources and developed a very simple system that works for me. If you desire to get your collectibles organized, here are a few helpful tips to get you started.

- ♫ Determine what method you will use to document your inventory. Use a 4x 6 index card writing information on one side and attaching photo on the backside. Or a three ring binder using notebook paper, plastic sleeves for photos & receipts and indexed dividers to separate by categories. If you are computer savvy develop an excel spreadsheet or purchase commercial software designed to database collectibles.

- ♫ Decide what information is important to document. These are called inventory elements. Sample elements include; item name, manufacturer & year, purchase price & date, or who gave you the item (such as birthday gift from Aunt Bessie). Record everything you know and be as specific as possible.

- ♫ Decide what organizational categories you will use. There are broad categories such as dolls, planters, and toys and sub-categories such as musical collectibles. If sub-categories are used be sure to cross reference this in your filing system.

- ♫ If you choose a commercial software product, be sure it is customizable so there is the flexibility to add elements that you deem important and the ability attach a photo.

- ♫ Photograph each item, preferably using a digital camera so you see the results immediately and retake if necessary.

- ♫ Catalog as you acquire. Resist the temptation to immediately display. Store new purchases/gifts in one area until the inventory process is complete.

Gathering and maintaining an organized collectibles inventory can be just as much fun as collecting. Handling each item, researching its origin and documenting as much information as you can, will enhance your enjoyment of all things Raggedy! Develop a system that works for you and start today!

About the Author

   Originally from Alabama, Karen resides in northwest Florida, with her husband of more than thirty years. She is a registered nurse and has a degree in business. Karen works as a program analyst for Navy Medicine, facilitating strategic planning and managing the programs of quality management, risk management, and customer relations. In her leisure time, she loves photography, scrap booking, vacationing at Walt Disney World, playing with her grandchildren, and searching for Raggedy Ann and Andy collectibles in flea markets and antique malls. Reuniting with her childhood doll twenty-eight years ago started her collecting frenzy, which has grown to number in the thousands, and at times has consumed every room in her home.